Tomorrow You Can

DOROTHY COREY

Pictures by Lois Axeman

ALBERT WHITMAN & Company, Chicago

Library of Congress Cataloging in Publication Data

Corey, Dorothy.
  Tomorrow you can.

  (A Self-starter book)
  SUMMARY: Pictures and brief text reassure small
children that soon they will be capable of doing many
things: tying shoes, sharing toys, and going off to
school.
    1.   Child development—Juvenile literature.
[1.   Child development] I. Axeman, Louis.   II. Title.
HQ767.9.C67   155.4'23   77-12789
ISBN 0-8075-8015-5

Text © 1977 by Dorothy Corey   Illustrations © 1977 by Lois Axeman
Published simultaneously in Canada by George J. McLeod, Limited, Toronto

If, today, you can't —

Maybe tomorrow you can.

Today.

Tomorrow.

Today

— and tomorrow.

Today,

tomorrow.

If you can't today,

maybe soon you can.

Today you can't.

Tomorrow you can.

Today you can't.

Tomorrow you can.

If you can't today,

maybe tomorrow

you can.

You can cut,

and tie,

— and go, and read,

and do so much!

You will be older

and braver.

You will be stronger,

—and bigger tomorrow.

If, today, you can't —

soon you can.

Tomorrow!

You can do so much!